How To Meditate

The Use-Anywhere Guide To
Eliminating Stress and Worry
Through Relaxation and Meditation

The Little Book That Gets Big Results

Steven Williams Chopra, M.D.

NMD Books
Simi Valley, CA

Visit our Web site at http://www.NMDbooks.com.

Library of Congress Cataloging-in-Publication Data
How to Meditate by Steven Williams Chopra
Includes bibliographical references and index.
ISBN: 978-0-9706773-9-6 (Softcover)

First Edition August 2010

Table of Contents:

What Is Meditation

Meditation is the practice and process of paying attention and focusing your awareness. When you meditate, a number of desirable things begin to happen — slowly, at first, and deepening over time.

First, when you can focus your awareness, you gain more power. When you concentrate any form of energy, including mental energy, you gain power.

When you focus your mind, you concentrate better. When you concentrate better, you perform better. You can accomplish more, whether in the classroom, in the boardroom, or in the athletic arena.

Whatever you do, you can do it more effectively when you meditate.

It is for this reason that spiritual teachers and texts often caution that one should begin the practice of meditation only in the context of other spiritual practices and disciplines that help develop compassion and wisdom to use properly this increased power.

Second, you enjoy your senses more fully. Although people sometimes view or use meditation as an ascetic experience to control their senses, meditation also can enhance your senses in ways that are profoundly sensual.

Anything that you enjoy — food, sex, music, art, massage, and so on — is greatly enhanced by meditation.

When you pay attention to something, it's a lot more enjoyable. Also, you don't need as much of it to get the same degree of pleasure, so you are more likely to enjoy without excess.

When you keep a wall around your heart to armor and protect it from pain, you also diminish your capacity to feel pleasure. When your life is in a continual rush, you may miss exquisite pleasures that exist from moment to moment.

Attention spans get shorter. The need for stimulation continually increases just to feel anything. Meditation increases awareness and sensitivity; as such, it can be an antidote to numbness and distraction.

Third, your mind quiets down and you experience an inner sense of peace, joy, and well being. When I first learned to meditate and began getting glimpses of inner peace, this experience changed my life.

It redefined and reframed my experience. Before, I thought piece of mind came from getting and doing; now, I understand that it comes from being.

It is our true nature to be peaceful until we disturb it.

This is a radically different concept of where our happiness and our well-being come from. In one of life's great paradoxes, not being aware of this truth, we often end up disturbing our inner peace while striving to get or to do what we think will bring that same peace to us.

Fourth, you may directly experience and become more aware of the transcendent interconnectedness that already exists. You may have a direct experience of God or the universal Self whatever name you give to this experience.

Meditation is simple in concept but difficult to master. Fortunately, you don't have to master meditation to benefit from it. You just have to practice. No one ever really masters it completely, but even a few steps down that road can make a meaningful difference. It is the process of meditation that makes it so beneficial, not how well you perform.

Well, the truth is, you're going to follow the same path no matter how high up the mountain you want to go. The basic instructions remain the same — but you get to choose your destination.

Among the most popular stopping places and promontories en route to the summit are the following:

• Stronger focus and concentration

• Reduced tension, anxiety, and stress

• Clearer thinking and less emotional turmoil

• Lower blood pressure and cholesterol

• Support in kicking addictions and other self-defeating behaviors

• Greater creativity and enhanced performance in work and play

• Increased self-understanding and self-acceptance

• More joy, love, and spontaneity

• Greater intimacy with friends and family members

• Deeper sense of meaning and purpose

• Glimpses of a spiritual dimension of being

As you can see, these way stations are actually major destinations in their own right, and all of them are well worth reaching.

The following are a few of the stages you may pass through on the path to just being :

• Getting used to sitting still

• Developing the ability to turn your attention inward

• Struggling to focus your attention

• Being distracted again and again

• Becoming more focused

• Feeling more relaxed as you meditate

• Noticing fleeting moments when your mind settles down

• Experiencing brief glimpses of stillness and peace

How Is Meditation Used

The basic idea generally associated with why people meditate is that during our day we are constantly subjected to sensory input and our minds are always active in the process of thinking.

We read the newspaper, study books, write reports, engage in conversation, solve problems – our whole waking state is a series of normal activities. Typically, as we do these normal activities we engage in a constant mental commentary, sort of an inner "The Drama of Me." Usually people aren't fully aware of all the mental thought activity that we are constantly engaged in.

Meditation allows all this activity to settle down, and often results in the mind becoming more peaceful, calm and focused. In essence, meditation allows the awareness to become 'rejuvenated'.

Meditation can be considered a technique, or practice. It usually involves concentrating on an object, such as a flower, a candle, a sound or word, or the breath. Over time, the number of random thoughts occurring diminishes. More importantly, your attachment to these thoughts, and your identification with them, progressively become less.

The meditator may get caught up in a thought pattern, but once he/she becomes aware of this, attention is gently brought back to the object of concentration. Meditation can also be objectless, for example consisting of just sitting.

Experiences during meditation probably vary significantly from one individual to another, or at least if different techniques are involved. Relaxation, increased awareness, mental focus and clarity, and a sense of peace are the most common by-products of meditation.

While much has been written about the benefits of meditation, the best attitude is not to have any expectations when practicing. Having a sense of expectation of (positive) results is likely to create unnecessary strain in the practice.

As well, since meditation involves becoming more aware and more sensitive to what is within you, facing unpleasant parts of oneself may well be part of meditation. Regardless of the experience, the meditator should try to be aware of the experience and of any attachment to it.

Failure to experience silence, peace of mind, mental clarity, bliss, or other promoted benefit of meditation is not in itself a sign of incorrect practice or that one can't concentrate properly or concentrate enough to be good at meditation.

Whether one experiences peace or bliss is not what is important.

What is generally considered important in meditation is that one is regular with their meditation -every day- and that one make a reasonable effort, but not strain, to remain with the object of concentration during the practice. With regular practice one inevitably acquires an increased understanding of and proficiency with the particular meditation technique.

Some people use the formal concentrative meditation as a preliminary step to practicing a mindfulness meditation during the day where one tries to maintain a calm but increased awareness of one's thoughts and actions during the day.

For some people, meditation is primarily a spiritual practice, and in some cases the meditation practice may be closely tied to the practice of a religion such as, for example, Hinduism or Buddhism.

Common Questions Answered

How is meditation different from relaxation, thinking, concentration or self-hypnosis?

Relaxation: Relaxation is a common by-product of meditation. Relaxation itself can assume many forms, such as taking a hot bath or reclining in the Lazy-boy and watching TV, etc. Meditation is an active process where the meditator remains fully aware of what the awareness is doing.

It also attempts to transcend the thought process whereas many forms of relaxation still engage the thought process. Meditation allows the body to relax and can offset the effects of stress both mentally and physically to a potentially much greater degree than passive relaxation.

Thinking: Thoughts generally consume energy in the process of their formation. Constant thought-activity, especially of random nature, can tire the mind and even bring on headache.

Meditation attempts to transcend this crude level of thought activity. Through regular practice one becomes aware that they are not their thoughts but that there is an awareness that exists independent of thought. Descartes ("I think, therefore I am") obviously was not a regular meditator!

Concentration: Meditation begins with concentration, but after an initial period of concentration, thought activity decreases and keeping the awareness focused becomes more spontaneous. At this point the person may or may not continue to employ the object of concentration.

Self-hypnosis: Self-hypnosis, like meditation, involves at least an initial period of concentration on an object. However in hypnosis one does not try to maintain an awareness of the here-and-now, or to stay conscious of the process. Instead one essentially enters a sort of semi-conscious trance.

What are the different meditation techniques?

Meditation involves concentrating on something to take our attention beyond the random thought activity that is usually going on in our heads. This can involve a solid object or picture, a mantra, breath, or guided visualization.

Typical objects employed include a candle flame or a flower. Some people use pictures, such as a mandala – a highly colored symmetric painting - or a picture of a spiritual teacher in a high meditative state. Mantras are sounds, which have a flowing, meditative quality and may be repeated out loud or inwardly. The breath is also a common focal point.

Finally, guided visualization is also considered by some to be a form of meditation. A guided visualization can help to bring one into a meditative state; also, visualization may be used once a meditative state has been reached to produce various results.

Which is right for me?

There is no "right" meditation technique for everybody.

Some techniques work better for certain people while other techniques work better for other people. The important thing is to find what works for you.

What are the abc's of meditation?

There are a few recommended guidelines for meditation:

• It should be done every day, preferably at the same time

• It should preferably be done before a meal rather than after a meal

• A spot should be set aside for meditation, which should be a quiet place and used for nothing but meditation

• One should sit with the spine straight and vertical (a chair is ok to use)

Is there any religious implication or affiliation with meditation?

Meditation has been and still is a central practice in eastern religions, for contacting "God" or one's higher Self. Christianity also has semblances of meditation, such as the biblical statement, "The kingdom of heaven is within you". Churches have a meditative atmosphere.

Meditation deals with contacting something within us that is peaceful, calm, rejuvenating, and meaningful. Whether one calls this something "God" or "soul" or "the inner child" or "theta-wave activity" or "peace" or "silence" is not important. It is there and anyone can benefit from it regardless of what they believe.

Most people in the world have already meditated. If you have relaxed looking at a beautiful sunset, allowing your thoughts to quiet down, this is close to meditation. If you have been reading a book for awhile, then put it down to take a break and just sat there quietly and peacefully for a few minutes without thinking, this is close to meditation.

Does meditation have any ethical implications?

In many traditions meditation practice is a means for reinforcing ethical qualities. In these traditions, calmness of mind, peacefulness and happiness are possible in meditation and in life generally only if they are accompanied by the observance of ethical norms of behavior.

What is the best time of day to meditate?

While meditation is beneficial at any time, most people who meditate agree that early morning is the best time to meditate. Part of the reason is that it is said that in early morning the hustle-and-bustle of the world has not yet begun and so it is easier to establish a meditative atmosphere. Having an early morning meditation also lets us carry some of the energy and peace of the meditation into our daily activities.

Many people also meditate either before dinner or later in the evening. Others also meditate at noon. A short meditation at these times allows one to throw off some of the accumulated stress of the work-day and become rejuvenated for further activity.

An important consideration is when your schedule will allow you to meditate. Having a time of the day set aside for meditation helps in maintaining regularity.

Why do some people use music while meditating?

Meditative music can help in establishing a meditative atmosphere. Also, some people find meditation relatively easy but find that the hard thing is to actually get themselves to sit down and start their meditation.

Music can help make this easier. Some people use music quite often while others prefer silent meditation and never use it.

Should I meditate with my eyes open or with my eyes closed?

Different traditions give different answers. Closing your eyes may contribute to drowsiness and sleepiness--if that's the case for you then try opening them a little. Opening your eyes may be distracting.

If that's the case try closing your eyes or direct your gaze on a blank wall (Zen-style). Or try with the eyes open halfway or a bit more, the gaze unfocussed and directed downward, but keeping the head erect with the chin slightly tucked in.

Sometimes meditators experience headaches from focusing on a spot too close to the eyes (perhaps closer than three feet). Whether focused or unfocussed, the gaze should be relaxed in order to prevent eyestrain or headache.

Experiment and see what works for you and then stick with your choice of technique. If you are using a candle, flower, or other visual object in your meditation then here the technique itself requires your eyes to be at least partly open.

What are the physiological effects of meditation?

The most common physiological effects of meditation are reduced blood pressure, lower pulse rate, decreased metabolic rate and changes in the concentration of serum levels of various substances.

When I meditate I experience physical pain in my body. What should I do?

Sensations (itching/aches/pains/etc.) can arise in the body when meditating for several reasons. Sometimes the cause is just an uncomfortable posture--make sure that your posture is comfortable under normal circumstances. Other times the cause is that sensations in the body are more noticeable in meditation.

The body and mind are calmer and you are able to notice more details in your bodily experience. It is often interesting to simply observe these sensations in your body: to use them as the objects of meditation. Sometimes these sensations just go away without your having to move or change your posture.

Remember that a quiet body contributes to a quiet mind.

How long should I meditate?

When first learning meditation it is usually not possible to meditate for more than 10-15 minutes. After regular practice for awhile, one becomes able to meditate for longer periods of time. Many people meditate twice-daily for 20-30 minutes each time, but the right duration and frequency is for each individual to decide.

Do I need a teacher?

It is theoretically possible to learn meditation from a book. However most people who teach and practice meditation agree that a teacher can be an invaluable aid in learning a meditation technique and making sure it is practiced correctly.

The beginner will usually have several questions, which a teacher will be able to answer. Also, learning with a group of people, e.g. a meditation class, allows you to experience the benefit of meditating with a group of people. Most people find that they have some of their best meditations while meditating in a group, because there is a collective energy and focus present.

Various individuals and groups teach meditation. Some charge and some do not. Many different techniques are taught, some more spiritual in nature and others mainly concerned with stress-reduction and gaining a little peace of mind. As always, the important thing is finding what works for you.

A Brief History of Meditation

It is unknown when the history of meditation began on Earth, let alone in Western civilization. Mountains could meditate, for all we know. Meditation was probably one of the oldest forms of mind control and self-healing. Meditation has been part of almost all ancient religious and magical traditions. The Native Americans practiced meditation and mindfulness, but called it by different names.

The Puritan Work Ethic

Mediation seemed to have fallen out of favor with the rise of Protestantism, particularly with the sect known as the Puritans. The Puritans are perhaps most famous for the Salem witchcraft trials in 1692 in Massachusetts. Puritans had a profound affect on the collective unconsciousness of the modern European or American. They believed in being busy all of the time. The only excuse you had for not being busy was death.

The history of meditation in Western civilization was also greatly affected by the Age of Enlightenment, which questioned the existence of a God and of all superstitions, anything new was encouraged. Anything old that didn't have a monetary value attached to it began to fall out of favor. When the Puritan work ethic coupled with this love of the new, meditation was considered to be stupid. This was a dark time and tense time in the history of meditation.

The Beatles

And thus we jump to 1967, when the Beatles really were more popular than Jesus. This is the crucial year in the history of meditation in the west. Although meditation in various forms was lectured on, written about and practiced here and there in all Western countries, it was considered a very odd thing to do.

But when the Beatles studied transcendental meditation (TM), their legions of fans became curious about what they were up to. They began to practice meditation, too. Because of the Beatles, meditation was opened up to everyone and entered the popular mindset. Meditation became just another normal part of life.

Today

We need meditation now just as in the dawn of the history of meditation. We are going through such unprecedented change in technology, sciences and cultural exchanges that we need to find some sort of anchor in the chaos. Meditation has helped many people get that anchor. Meditation is encouraged for anyone, from Catholic nuns to atheists.

Although we do not know what the future of meditation holds, it will likely be around for as long as there are thinking beings. The popular science fiction series Star Trek had the incredibly intelligent alien race of Vulcans be habitual meditators.

Common Myths About Meditation

The Top Ten Myths About Meditation

Even though meditation is now widely used in sports, medicine, psychiatry, and of course as part of the spiritual practice of millions of people around the world, there are still many misconceptions in circulation about what meditation actually is.

Myth #10. - Meditation is relaxation

To say that some people's conception of meditation is "Think of warm puppies, and let your mind go limp" is an exaggeration, but not much of one. Perhaps because meditation has found a home in stress management classes around the world, many people think that "letting your tensions dissolve away" is the be-all and end-all of a meditation practice.

But while it's important to let go of unnecessary effort while meditating, meditation is still a practice — that is, it involves effort. Sure, we start by letting go of tensions in the body, but that's only the start.

Myth #9. - Meditation is just self-hypnosis

Hypnosis, when used in therapy, involves a patient being guided into having experiences that he or she would have difficulty in attaining unaided — experiences as varied as being content without a cigarette in hand and remembering forgotten events from childhood.

Self-hypnosis does the same thing, but the practitioner uses a remembered script or visualization to, say, increase relaxation or to experience greater confidence. There's actually some overlap between hypnosis and meditation (although some meditation teachers, being suspicious of hypnosis, would deny this).

In both disciplines we start with inducing a state of relaxation and then proceed to doing some kind of inner work. In hypnosis and in some forms of meditation that inner work involves visualization or the use of repeated phrases. But many forms of meditation (for example, Zen "just sitting" or Theravadin mindfulness meditation) make no use of such tools. The overlap between hypnosis and meditation is only partial.

Myth #8 There Are Technological Shortcuts

"I want to relax, and I want to do it now!" is the approach taken by many goal-oriented Westerners. And that makes them suckers for promises of quick-fix technological approaches to meditating. The web is full of products that promise you that you'll meditate like a Zen monk at the touch of a button.

Just stick your headphones on and hit play, and let the magical audio technology do the rest! But like myth #10, this overlooks the fact that meditation involves effort. Sure, if you stop running around being stressed for half an hour and listen to some blandly pleasant music you'll find you're more relaxed. Why wouldn't you be?

But it's a mistake to confuse this with real meditation. The "Zen monk" in these ads would surely be puzzled to think that someone listening to a CD for a few minutes had attained the depths of mindfulness and compassion that come from thousands of hours of sitting on a cushion watching your breath.

Myth #7 - Transcendental Meditation Is The Most Common Kind of Meditation

"Oh, so is it Transcendental meditation you do?" I've lost count of the number of times I've been asked that question when people have found out I'm a meditation teacher. Just about everyone has heard of Transcendental Meditation because of famous practitioners like the Beatles and because of controversies about TM being taught in U.S. schools, but TM is very much a minority pursuit — probably because it's so darned expensive to learn (and the question of where those millions of dollars go is still open).

The most common form of meditation in the West is Mindfulness or Insight meditation, which comes from Theradavin Buddhism of South and Southeast Asia. Zen meditation and Tibetan meditation (which often involves visualization) isn't far behind.

Myth #6 - You Have To Sit In Lotus Position

In the Asian countries where Buddhist meditation developed people generally sit on the floor and have flexible hips. It's natural for them to sit cross-legged, and so they sit in a variety of cross-legged postures in order to meditate, the lotus position being one of the most common and stable postures.

In the West we sit in chairs from an early age and have stiffer hips. It's therefore a rare Westerner who can sit in the lotus position to meditate — at least with any degree of comfort. In actual fact it's possible to sit comfortably to meditate on a chair, a meditation stool, kneeling, or even lying down (although you'll have trouble staying awake).

The most important thing is that you find a posture that's comfortable for you — and that you don't beat yourself up about not being able to twist your legs like a pretzel.

Myth #5 - In Meditation You Sit There Saying "OM"

Mantra meditation is only one kind of meditation, and "OM" is only one mantra (or part of a mantra). 'Nuff said.

Myth #4 - Meditation Is A Religious Activity

Although meditation comes from various spiritual or religious traditions, it's not in itself necessarily a religious practice. The most common forms of meditation practice, for example, involve observing the sensations of the breath. What's religious about that?

Sure, there are some forms of meditation that involve using religious words of phrases as objects of concentration (e.g. Transcendental Meditation, Buddhist Mantra meditation, etc.) but many of the most common meditation practices have no religious overtones — which is probably one of the reasons they're so common.

Myth #3 - Meditation Is Somehow "Eastern"

A lot of people (usually Christians) have told me that they think Buddhist practice is "foreign" because it comes from an Eastern context. Hmm, where does Christianity come from again? Oh yes, the Middle East. But as with Myth #4 ("Meditation is a religious activity") there's nothing inherently Eastern, Southern, or Northern about counting your breath or wishing people well.

Some Tibetan practices do involve visualizing rather bizarre (to Western eyes) figures, and mantra meditation usually involves repeating Sanskrit words or phrases — but those constitute a minority of meditation practices. Oh, all right, it's a large minority — but what's wrong with a little exoticism?

Myth #2 - Meditation Is Escapist

To some people, meditation is "running away from problems," "navel gazing," "lotus eating," or "disregarding the world." Actually, running around being busy and never having time to experience yourself deeply is escapism. When you meditate you're brought face-to-face in a very direct way with your own anger, delusion, craving, pain, and selfishness.

There's nothing to do in meditation but to experience and work with these things. Also, some forms of meditation — such as loving kindness and compassion meditation — involve us working at transforming our relationship with the world by cultivating love and empathy for others.

Perhaps that's why so many meditators are involved in social work, psychotherapy, nursing, bereavement counseling, prison work, etc.

Myth #1 - Meditation Is About Letting Your Mind Go Blank

Here it is, the all-time number one meditation myth — that meditation is about "making your mind go blank." Sure, in meditation we aim to reduce the amount of thinking that goes on.

Sure, just sit there for a few minutes watching all those pointless and even downright unhelpful thoughts bubbling up nonstop in the mind and you'd start to think that a blank mind would be preferable! But what would it be like to have a blank mind?

Would you even be awake? Would you have any consciousness at all? Would you be able to know that your mind was blank? The confusion arises because we identify so much with our verbal thoughts (our inner self-talk) that we think that that's all our experience is. And if we reduce or even stop our thinking (and that can happen) we assume that the mind must be blank. But a blank mind simply isn't possible.

No, in meditation we aim to develop mindfulness — that's mind-full-ness. When we're mindful the mind is very much not blank. Rather, we're aware of physical sensations, emotions, thoughts — and of how all those things interact with each other.

The mind is so full of our present-moment experience that there's less room for it to be full of useless thoughts, and instead we're aware of the incredible richness of our experience — a richness that we overlook entirely when we spend our whole lives lost in thinking.

Practical Meditation In The Modern World

Is it practical to try and practice and achieve bliss in a frantic modern world filled with so many distractions? Absolutely, and it is for this very reason we are in need of its comfort and solace.

In many cases we choose to be distracted. Keeping the TV on tuned to news channels; the radio in the car tuned to Talk Radio; leaving our pagers and cell phones on so we can be distracted from anything and everything are just a few examples of how we choose to be distracted.

When we practice meditation, we are encouraged to block out the distractions of everyday life, and we can learn from the practice of minimizing distraction.

Even when you are not meditating, try these simple techniques to have less distraction in your life:

- Leave your cell phone and pager off and return messages the same time each day.

- Leave the TV off during the evenings and play soothing gentle music or go with silence instead.

- Use voice mail for your home phone and leave the ringer turned off and answer your messages in the mornings only or at a given time each day.

Eliminating Stress, Worry and Anxiety Through Meditation

For me, being rid of anxiety, worry and stress gets down to developing a general philosophy of being that centers around acceptance of what is.

When you think about it, much of our dissonance and stress comes from longing and desiring and wanting things to be different than what they are right now in this moment.

"If only things were different, I'd be happy."

But history shows that when people get what they want they are not happy anyway, and therein lies the conundrum of the human condition.

The answer to this "existential dilemma" is simply this:

If you stay in the moment and simply accept "what is" and not try to change it, then you are on your way toward mental freedom.

To accept things as they are and allow things to unfold as they will unfold and be detached from their outcomes is the basis of many world religions and philosophies, and when it gets right down to it, much of what happens to us or will happen to us is beyond our control, so why fret about it?

I adopt a philosophy I call DOA.

Detach – Observe – Allow.

I start with this frame of mind when I begin to meditate to clear my mind of worries and thoughts about past and future and real or imagined fears.

Much of what we fear is in the acronym of FEAR:

False Evidence Appearing Real.

The Power of Belief

Ever heard the story of the four-minute mile? For years people believed that it is impossible for a human being to run a mile in less than four minutes until Roger Banister proved it wrong in 1954. Within one year, 37 runners broke the belief barrier. And the year after that, 300 other runners did the same thing.

What happens if you put an animal in a pond? Any animal, big or small, will swim its way through. What happens when someone, who does not know how to swim, falls in deep waters? You drown. If an animal who has not learned swimming could escape by swimming, why not you? Because you believe you will drown while the animal does not.

You have used a computer keyboard or a typewriter.

Ever wondered why the alphabets are organized in a particular order in your keyboard? You might have thought it is to increase the typing speed. Most people never question it. But the fact is that this system was developed to reduce the typing speed at a time when typewriter parts would jam if the operator typed too fast.

These three cases show the power of our beliefs. There is no other more powerful directing force in human behavior than belief. Your beliefs have the power to create and to destroy. A belief delivers a direct command to your nervous system.

Have you heard about the placebo effect? People who are told a drug will have a certain effect will many times experience that effect even when given a pill without those properties.

It is also our belief that determines how much of our potential we will be able to tap. So you better examine some of your beliefs minutely. For example, do you believe that you can excel in whatever you do? Do you believe you are bad in mathematics? Do you believe that other people don't like you? Do you believe life is full of problems? What are your beliefs about people?

No belief is right or wrong. It is either empowering or limiting. A belief is nothing but the generalization of a past incident. As a kid if a dog bit you, you believed all dogs to be dangerous. To change a particular behavior pattern, identify the beliefs associated with it. Change those beliefs and a new pattern is automatically created.

Simple Meditation Techniques

Meditation is simply the practice of focusing your attention on a particular object - generally something simple, like a word or phrase, a candle flame or geometrical figure, or the coming and going of your breath.

In everyday life, your mind is constantly processing a barrage of sensations, visual impressions, emotions, and thoughts. When you meditate, you narrow your focus, limit the stimuli bombarding your nervous system — and calm your mind in the process.

To get a quick taste of meditation, follow these instructions as 5-step process:

Meditation Technique #1

1. Find a quiet place and sit comfortably with your back relatively straight. If you tend to

disappear into your favorite chair, find something a bit more supportive.

2. Take a few deep breaths, close your eyes, and relax your body as much as you can. If you don't know how to relax, you may try sitting, laying or whatever comfortable for you.

3. Choose a word or phrase that has special personal or spiritual meaning for you. Here are some examples: "There's only love," "Don't worry, be happy," "Trust in God."

4. Begin to breathe through your nose (if you can), and as you breathe, repeat the word or phrase quietly to yourself. You can whisper the word or phrase, sub-vocalize it (that is, move your tongue as though saying it, but not aloud), or just repeat it in your mind. If you get distracted, come back to the repetition of the word or phrase.

As an alternative, you can follow your breath as it comes and goes through your nostrils, returning to your breathing when you get distracted.

5. Keep the meditation going for five minutes or more; then slowly get up and go about your day.

Meditation Technique #2

This is my favorite technique, one I learned from the guided meditation CD "Music for Relaxation and Deep Meditation put out by a company called MindWaves.

1. Lie down comfortably on the bed in a room where you will have no distractions. If possible, darken the room or reduce the amount of light.

2. As you lie comfortably: Take a deep breath, drawing in air for a count of five. Hold the air in your lungs for a count of five. Now slowly exhale. Again… (Do three times.)

3. Now breathe normally, being aware of your breath. As you become aware of your breath, clear your mind of all thoughts. Your mind is a blank dark screen.

4. Thoughts will come and go, as they do, let them go, flowing out of you as quickly as they come in.

5. Focus the attention on the area in the middle of your forehead just above your eyes. Be aware of your breathing.

6. You are slowly becoming more relaxed, your body is letting go, becoming heavier and

heavier as you sink deeper into the bed, deeper into relaxation.

7. Imagine your spirit, your inner core, your inner light is a whirling ball of white light, a whirling sphere of energy, as it lengthens and expands the length of your entire being and permeates every cell, energizing your being with relaxing karmic light and warmth.

This wonderful warmth and light is expanding into every cell, every fiber of your being. You are sinking deeper and deeper into relaxation toward sleep.

8. As you do your thoughts are quiet, you are no longer identified with the material self, you are now only the spiritual self, the being of pure white light.

There is no past or future, only the present of the moment of now and in that moment there is no identification with self, memories or reflections, only the present awareness of the now moment.

9. That now moment is pure light, pure energy – bliss - peace – serenity. You are a pillar of white light now channeling the cosmic energy of the universe through you – a circuit for joy – love - peace.

10. You will not visualize any concept or result of this awareness, only hold the pure awareness of now and the light in your consciousness.

11. Deeper you go into relaxation toward sleep.

12. In this deep state of awareness you will repeat your goals and affirmations as you instruct the infinite power of your subconscious mind to be receptive to them as the one true reality.

While you sleep, the affirmations you have given your subconscious mind will manifest as the one and only true reality.

How did you feel? Did it seem weird to say the same thing or follow your breath over and over? Did you find it difficult to stay focused? Did you keep changing the phrase? If so, don't worry.

With regular practice and the guidance of this book, you'll gradually get the knack. Of course, you could easily spend many fruitful and enjoyable years mastering the subtleties and complexities of meditation.

But the good news is, the basic practice is actually quite simple, and you don't have to be an expert to do it — or to enjoy its extraordinary benefits.

The main thing to remember is not to get hung up on technique. Any technique in which you quiet your mind and are still is meditation.

Experiment with what works best for you.

Some like to meditate sitting in a lotus position, some in an Indian style position, some like to lie down on bed, some in a chair with their back straight and hand resting comfortably on their knees.

All are perfectly acceptable.

The location is another variable that you may experiment with. I like to go into my bedroom closet when I want total silence, but much of the time just lying down on the bed works for me.

Basic Relaxation Meditation

For this one lying on the floor is actually best. Please try not to fall asleep though! Put your palms down on the floor by your sides. Your feet should be just a few inches apart.

OK. Now just lie still for a few seconds. Let your thoughts gradually quiet down. Without any force at all let your breathing becomes naturally deep and regular. Now feel the weight of your body on the floor.

Now we're going to very quickly just 'name' some parts of the body in turn. Center your consciousness briefly on each of these parts as you name them to yourself. Toes, feet, ankles, calves, knees, thoughts, groin, midriff, chest, shoulders, hands, arms, neck and head. Be aware of any areas where there is particular tension. OK? Now I'll just explain the next bit before we do it.

What we're going to do is spend five seconds making our whole bodies as tense as we possibly can. Then we're going to release all of that tension in one go, pushing it out and up and away from us. But before we do this, on the count of three take a long deep breath in. One, two, three -now tense as many muscles in your body as you possibly can, and when I count three push the air in your lungs out at the same time as you let go of every last little bit of that tension. One, two, three - push away the stress!

Now concentrate on your breathing. Breathing in through the nose and out through the nose is best here, but find some other way if that is uncomfortable for you. Let your breaths be deep, and let your mind be still. Just watch the way you take in the air and how it fills your lungs. Hold the air in your lungs for just for a second or two before you breathe out, and wait for just a second or two before you breathe in again. Just watch your breath for thirty seconds or so. If you get distracted or your mind wanders, then gently bring it back.

Now try and maintain the sense that by letting the body relax, and by allowing the mind to be still, so you are letting all parts of the system become more integrated. By simply being calm, and aware, you are letting bodymind become more balanced. More efficient. More energized. Be calm in this attitude for another minute or so.

Now gradually bring yourself out of the meditation, slowly bringing your attention back to where you are.

Zen Meditation

Zen meditation allows the mind to relax, please follow theses easy instructions. Sit on the forward third of a chair or a cushion on the floor.

Arrange your legs in a position you can maintain comfortably. In the half-lotus position, place your right leg on your left thigh.

In the full lotus position, put your feet on opposite thighs. You may also sit simply with your legs tucked in close to your body, but be sure that your weight is distributed on three points: both of your knees on the ground and your buttocks on the round cushion. On a chair, keep your knees apart about the width of your shoulders, feet firmly planted on the floor.

Take a deep breath, exhale fully, and take another deep breath, exhaling fully.

With proper physical posture, your breathing will flow naturally into your lower abdomen. Breathe naturally, without judgment or trying to breathe a certain way.

Keep your attention on your breath whilst practicing this Zen meditation. When your attention wanders, bring it back to the breath again and again -- as many times as necessary! Remain as still as possible, following your breath and returning to it whenever thoughts arise.

Be fully, vitally present with yourself. Simply do your very best. At the end of your sitting period, gently swing your body from right to left in increasing arcs. Stretch out your legs, and be sure they have feeling before standing.

Practice easy Zen meditation every day for at least ten to fifteen minutes (or longer) and you will discover for yourself the treasure house of the timeless life of zazen -- your very life itself.

Here and Now Meditation

Now I am going to describe a meditation technique which is one of the most effective and easiest meditation techniques of all times. Here is a technique which you can perform anytime, anywhere and in any position. .

I hope by now you know what is meditation (if not please see what is meditation). In order to understand this technique let us recall the meaning of meditation.

Meditation is a systematic way of making our mind quiet so that we can contact our true identity -self, which is the source of everlasting joy, bliss and peace.

This state in which our mind becomes absolutely calm and relaxed is also known as the state of choiceless awareness i.e. the state where we are fully aware of the moment yet our awareness is not focused on any physical or mental image/object. It is a choiceless awareness. In the 'Here and now' meditation we will gradually achieve the state of choiceless awareness with the help of three easy steps. For the sake of simplicity I am referring these steps as three individual steps. In reality as you perform these steps, you will realize that these three steps happens simultaneously and thus are parts of one single step.

The three steps of 'here and now' meditation technique are:

(1) Remind yourself that you exist here and now.

This will make you aware of your body as it exists here and now.

(2) Just be aware of the activities going on in and around you at this moment.

This will make you aware of the universe as it exists here and now.

(3) From now onwards start doing everything with awareness.

This will make you aware you of yourself as it exists here and now.

Let us understand these three steps is detail:

First step:

"Remind yourself that you exist here and now."

Remind yourself that you exist here and now. I am using the word ' remind' because most of us tend to forget that we, in reality, exist here and now. We exist in the present. Nobody can live in past or future. Whatever we do, feel, think or experience, we do it in the present moment. You may think about past, you may plan for the future but the very process (of thinking about past or planning for the future) always happens in the present because at any given moment you exist in the present.

Your existence in this world is the sum total of many things. Your present personality is the combined result of your physical makeup, your cultural, social and educational background, your thoughts, your feelings, your past life, your future plans, your ambitions and desires etc. However, you, who is the combined embodiment of all such varied factors, exist here and now - in the present moment! You can escape from the past, you can evade the outcome of future but you can not escape from the present. Most of us just keep thinking about the memories of past or fancies of the future and give very little importance to present whereas one of the most important and fundamental requisite for meditation is that you should live in the present.

In order to meditate and make our mind quiet, it is important for us to accept our life as it exists in the present moment. No matter how boring, banal, stressful, sad or colorless our present life is; at any given moment, it is all that we have with us. So accept your life as it is and remind yourself that you exist in the present moment. The aim of this step is to focus your whole attention on the present moment. This initial step act as a launching pad for the 'here and now' meditation as the entire attention of the meditator get focused on the present moment. So: Just be aware of the fact that you exist here and now !

Second step:

"Just be aware of the activities going on in and around you at this moment."

At any given moment there are many things that are happening in and around you. Even if you are just sitting and not doing anything, many things are going on. Your breathing process is going on, your heart is pumping the blood and ensuring its circulation in body, the digestion process is going on inside you, kidneys are filtering the blood, various glands in your body are secreting hormones to ensure proper metabolism of the body. Your hair and nails are growing at a small speed, in short - hundred of activities are going on inside your body at this very moment.

In the outer world also numerous things are happening around you at the present moment. You are surrounded by a very active atmosphere, whose properties such as temperature, pressure etc. are changing every moment. There are numerous sounds echoing around you at this very moment - movement of fan, ticking of clock, music in radio or your PC, conversation of people, rain drops outside the windows, the water you sip from the glass, sounds of your own movements etc all these phenomena are producing sound around you.

Well if you observe closely you will find yourself surrounded by a pool of various activities. This collective pool of activities constitutes the choreography of the universe as it unfolds itself every moment. Universe or creation is an ongoing phenomenon. It is a kind of cosmic dance that is going on. It's not only you who is surrounded by so many activities. Each and everyone among us is enfolded by this dance of universe. We seldom or never give our attention to these activities that goes on in and around us. However, the truth is that they keep happening on their own and produce an effect in our lives.

So in the second part of this meditation technique, you are required to become aware of this cosmic dance. Just be aware of the present moment. Just be aware of all those activities which are going on in and around you at this present moment. Do not concentrate upon them .Thing are happening on their own. Just be aware of them. Wind is blowing, machines are running, fan is moving, TV is on, music is coming from the radio, traffic is running on the roads, trains are running on tracks, dogs are barking, children are playing & fighting, hawkers are shouting to attract the customers. At any given moment the whole world is full of activities of every kind. . Just be aware of these activities. Don't contemplate over them. Don't try to make them a part of your thinking process. Just, at this very moment, be aware of this cosmic choreography. This step of becoming aware of the present moment helps the meditator in increasing the depth of his/her awareness.

After the first step of meditation (which requires you to be aware that you exist in the present moment), this second step will help you to be aware of the whole cosmos as it exists in the present moment. So just be aware of the activities which are going on in and around you at the present moment.

This moment is as it should be, because the whole universe is as it should be. The moment -- the one you're experiencing right now-- is the culmination of all the moments you have experienced in the past. This moment is as it is because the entire universe is as it is.

A relevant thought from: The seven spiritual laws of success by Deepak Chopra.

Third step:

"From now onwards start doing everything with awareness"

This step is the third and the most important step of this meditation technique. In the previous two steps you become aware of the present moment and of the cosmic chaos which exists at this moment. In this third step, you are not required to do anything special. Just keep doing whatever you are doing at this moment but ---- do it with awareness that you are doing it.

Let me explain what I mean:

If you are eating anything: eat it with awareness that you are eating something. Just be aware of every step you take in eating. Right from holding (say bread for example) in your hand, taking the bread towards your mouth, inserting it in your mouth, chewing the bread and swallowing it in mouth, just perform everything with awareness.

Same with drinking: Whatever you are drinking, drink it with absolute awareness of the process of drinking. If you drink a glass of water, drink it with full awareness while you hold the glass of water in your hand. Be aware of the sensation your hands feel on touching the glass, take the glass near your mouth with awareness, just be aware of every sip you take. After drinking, put back the glass with awareness.

If you walk, walk with awareness. While you walk, just be aware of the movements of body as you walk. If your right hands comes forward while you move your left leg, just be aware of this. If while walking in the garden you feel the urge to take a deep breath, take the long breath but take it with awareness.

Include this practice of awareness in all those process also where some kind of movement is not required. For example if you are not doing anything and just sitting somewhere, be aware of that (i.e. sitting), just have an awareness of your sitting posture, watch with awareness as your body changes it's position while sitting. Similarly, if you are lying on a bed, just be aware of the fact that you are lying. Have an awareness of the movements your body performs while lying on the bed.

Doing everything with awareness is something that can be done anytime, anywhere and in any posture. It does not require allocating some extra time or sitting in a particular place. Just start doing everything with awareness. It is very simple and you can do it right now.

If you drive, drive with awareness.

While bathing, take your bath with awareness, just be awareness of the sensation you feel when you pour water on your body. Just be aware of how it feels when you use the towel to rinse the body.

The main aim of this meditation is to break the habit of a mechanical life which most of us are living. We all have become some sort of robots. There is very little awareness left in us. Almost all our daily work such as eating, drinking, bathing, reading, playing, driving, talking, traveling, writing, listening, watching etc are done by us in a mechanical manner. In such a mechanical life, when we are not even performing very basic mundane tasks with awareness, how we can explore or know the awareness of our self?

This *Here and Now Meditation* aims to increase our overall awareness of everything. When you perform every task with awareness, slowly you will start recognizing the witness in you who watches everything as you perform the task. As your awareness increases, you will start becoming more and more aware of your true self.

As you keep practicing this meditation, after some time a stage will come when two distinct aspects of your identity will emerge: one - doing and another - being. You will be doing every work assigned to you, yet there will be some in you (the being aspect) who will remain intact as a watcher while you perform your work. This 'being aspect' is your true self. Once you realize this 'being aspect' you will realize the immortal part of your existence. You will realize the supreme consciousness.

This too will pass...

One Answer... for all questions

This meditation technique is quite different from those that I described earlier. This technique is actually a contemplation exercise and involves thinking over life. Though people of all age can try this technique, it is basically suitable for people with mature age (I mean 18 & above). The reason is that only those who have lived a certain (substantial) duration of life can reflect back on their past. Very young people who are still in the initial phase of their life are less likely (though not impossible) to analyze their life from the angle which this meditation demands. Nevertheless, this meditation technique is very useful for knowing our true self.

Method:

First read this thought provoking story:

Once a king called upon all of his wise men and asked them, "Is there a mantra or suggestion which works in every situation, in every circumstance, in every place and in every time, something which can help me when none of you is available to advise me. Tell me is there any mantra?"

All wise men got puzzled by King's question. One answer for all question? Something that works everywhere, in every situation? In every joy, every sorrow, every defeat and every victory? They thought and thought. After a lengthy discussion, an old man suggested something which appeals to all of them. They went to king and gave him something written on paper. But the condition was that king was not to see it out of curiosity. Only in extreme danger, when the King finds himself alone and there seems to be no way, only then he'll have to see it. The King put the papers under his Diamond ring.

After a few days, the neighbors attack the Kingdom. It was a collective surprise attack of King's enemies. King and his army fought bravely but lost the battle. King had to fled on his horse. The enemies were following him. His horse took him far away in Jungle. He could hear many troops of horses were following him and the noise was coming closer and closer.

Suddenly the King found himself standing in the end of the road - that road was not going anywhere. Underneath there was a rocky valley thousand feet deep. If he jumped into it, he would be finished…and he could not return because it was a small road… From back the sound of enemy's horses was approaching fast. King became restless. There seemed to be no way.

Then suddenly he saw the Diamond in his ring shining in the sun, and he remembered the message hidden in the ring. He opened the diamond and read the message. The message was very small but very great.

The message was - "This too will pass."

The King read it. Again read it. Suddenly something strike in his mind - Yes! it too will pass. Only a few days ago, I was enjoying my kingdom. I was the mightiest of all the Kings. Yet today, the Kingdom and all his pleasure have gone. I am here trying to escape from enemies. However when those days of luxuries have gone, this day of danger too will pass. A calm came on his face. He kept standing there.

The place where he was standing was full of natural beauty. He had never known that such a beautiful place was also a part of his Kingdom. The revelation of message had a great effect on him. He relaxed and forget about those following him. After a few minute he realized that the noise of the horses and the enemy coming was receding. They moved into some other part of the mountains and were not on that path.

The King was very brave. He reorganized his army and fought again. He defeated the enemy and regained his lost empire. When he returned to his empire after victory, he was received with much fan fare at the door.

The whole capital was rejoicing in the victory. Everyone was in a festive mood. Flowers were being thrown on King from every house, from every corner. People were dancing and singing. For a moment King said to himself," I am one of the bravest and greatest King. It is not easy to defeat me. With all the reception and celebration he saw an ego emerging in him.

Suddenly the Diamond of his ring flashed in the sunlight and reminded him of the message. He open it and read it again: "This too will pass"

He became silent. His face went through a total change - from the egoist he moved to a state of utter humbleness.

If this too is going to pass, it is not yours.

The defeat was not yours, the victory is not yours.

You are just a watcher. Everything passes by.

We are witness of all this. We are the perceiver. Life come and go. Happiness come and go. Sorrow come and go.

Now as you have read this story, just sit silently and evaluate your own life. This too will pass. Think of the moments of joy and victory in your life. Think of the moment of Sorrow and defeat. Are they permanent? They all come and pass away. Life just passes away.

There were friends in past. They all have gone.

There are friends today. They too will go.

There will be new friends tomorrow. They too will go.

There were enemies in past. They have gone.

There may be enemy in present. They too will go.

There will be new enemies tomorrow and… they too will go.

There is nothing permanent in this world. Every thing changes except the law of change. Think over it from your own perspective. You have seen all the changes. You have survived all setbacks, all defeats and all sorrows. All have passed away. If there are problems in the present, they too will pass away.

Because nothing remains forever. Joy and sorrow are the two faces of the same coin. They both will pass away. Who are you in reality? Know your real face. Your face is not your true face. It will change with the time. However, there is something in you, which will not change. It will remain unchanged. What is that unchangeable?

It is nothing but your true self.

You are just a witness of change. Experience it, understand it.

Everyday for 10-15 minutes sit in silence. Just think over the sentence, "This too will pass." Pondering over your own life will make you realize the true meaning of this sentence. Everything passes yet your real identity remains the same. That real you is your true self. To know that self is true meditation.

Simple Meditation

This meditation process is good to induce relaxation response. Plan to make meditation a regular part of your daily routine. Set aside 10 to 20 minutes each day at the same time, if possible. Before breakfast is a good time.

Choose a quiet spot where you will not be disturbed by other people or by the telephone.

Sit quietly in a comfortable position. Refer to the section on postures for recommendations on sitting positions.

Eliminate distractions and interruptions during the period you'll be meditating.

Commit yourself to a specific length of time and try to stick to it.

Pick a focus word or short phrase that's firmly rooted in your personal belief system. A non-religious person might choose a neutral word like one, peace, or love. Others might use the opening words of a favorite prayer from their religion such as 'Hail Mary full of Grace', "I surrender all to you", "Hallelujah", "Om", etc.

Close your eyes. This makes it easy to concentrate.

Relax your muscles sequentially from head to feet. This helps to break the connection between stressful thoughts and a tense body. Starting with your forehead, become aware of tension as you breathe in. Let go of any obvious tension as you breathe out. Go through the rest of your body in this way, proceeding down through your eyes, jaws, neck, shoulders, arms, hands, chest, upper back, middle back and midriff, lower back, belly, pelvis, buttocks, thighs, calves, and feet.

Breathe slowly and naturally, repeating your focus word or phrase silently as you exhale.

Assume a passive attitude. Don't worry about how well you're doing. When other thoughts come to mind, simply say, "Oh, well," and gently return to the repetition.

Continue for 10 to 20 minutes. You may open your eyes to check the time, but do not use an alarm. After you finish: Sit quietly for a minute or so, at first with your eyes closed, and later with your eyes open. Do not stand for one or two minutes.

Plan for a session once or twice a day.

Walking Meditation

According to Jon Kabat-Zinn Director of the Stress Reduction Clinic at the University of Massachusetts Medical Center, one simple way to bring awareness into your life is through walking meditation. "This brings your attention to the actual experience of walking as you are doing it, focusing on the sensations in your feet and legs, feeling your whole body moving, " Dr. Kabat-Zinn explains. "You can also integrate awareness of your breathing with the experience."

To do this exercise, focus the attention on each foot as it contacts the ground. When the mind wanders away from the feet or legs, or the feeling of the body walking, refocus your attention. To deepen your concentration, don't look around, but keep your gaze in front of you.

"One thing that you find out when you have been practicing mindfulness for a while is that nothing is quite as simple as it appears," says Dr. Kabat-Zinn. "This is as true for walking as it is for anything else. For one thing, we carry our mind around with us when we walk, so we are usually absorbed in our own thoughts to one extent or another.

We are hardly ever just walking, even when we are just going out for a walk'. Walking meditation involves intentionally attending to the experience of walking itself.

Transcendental Meditation

Transcendental Meditation is by far the most thoroughly researched in terms of its benefits for mental, physical, and social health TM is a simple mental technique, easy to learn and practice.
Anyone can learn it within a few days and can begin to experience beneficial results almost

immediately. Since 1958, 4 million people have learned TM and over five hundred scientific studies have been conducted on it at over two hundred universities worldwide.

TM is one of the easiest meditation techniques to learn. When you learn TM, an instructor gives you a word or phrase-your personal mantra-which you promise not to divulge. You are told to sit quietly with your eyes closed and repeat the mantra over and over again for 20 minutes at a time once or twice a day.

The mantra functions to focus your mind on a single idea, representing the "oneness" of the universe. You're instructed to assume a passive, accepting attitude while repeating your mantra. When distracting thoughts intrude, you're instructed to simply observe them, accept them and gently return your mental focus to repeating your mantra.

Physiological research shows that during TM, the body gains a deeper state of relaxation than during ordinary rest. EEG (electroencephalogram) changes indicate a state of heightened awareness and coherence.

Regular practice of TM has been found to produce a state of increased stability, adaptability, and integration during all phases of activity. Also, TM has been found to increase intelligence, creativity, and perceptual ability and to reduce high blood pressure and illness rates by more than 50 percent.

Analysis of large numbers of research studies on TM have found that it is one of the most effective techniques known for reducing drug and alcohol abuse, decreasing anxiety and increasing self-actualization.

Mindfulness (Vipassana)

In mantra and breath meditation, you focus on a word or your breath and try to empty your mind of everything else. This mental clearing is what most people mean when they refer to meditation.

But there's another kind of meditation, a practice Buddhists call vipassana or sometimes called mindfulness, or insight meditation. It is the art of becoming deeply aware of the present instant. Mindfulness means fully experiencing what happens in the here and now. It is the art of focusing our minds on what's happening in and around us at this very moment. Mindfulness helps you turn down all the noise in your head- the guilt, anger, doubts, and uncertainties that upset us moment to moment. It is a technique that encourages you to stop and smell the roses.

The key is not so much what you focus on but how you do it. What is more important is the quality of the awareness you bring to each moment. That awareness should be meditative in the sense of being a silent witness, accepting and nonjudgmental.

It, however, does not imply resignation to abuse or injustice. It teaches acknowledgment of the moment-to-moment reality and prepares those who use the technique to respond to that reality less impulsively and more effectively.

There are two kinds of mindful meditation - formal and informal. Yoga is a good example of the formal type. In a yoga class, participants focus intently on their breathing and the postures, moving slowly from one position to the next, exquisitely aware of their feelings during the process.

Practitioners are taught to concentrate on their breathing and its passage through the body as they dismiss any distracting thoughts. Though it sounds simple, mindfulness takes practice, and the longer you practice, the easier the process becomes. Breathing is the vehicle of transition from our conventional, anxiety-ridden, goal-oriented experience of stressful living into a natural state of functional calm and tranquility.

Tai chi offers a similar dimension of mindfulness. Informal mindfulness involves turning the headlong rush of daily living into a collection of discrete moments of experience, each savored fully. For example, Dr. Kabat-Zinn hands each of his students a single raisin and asks them to eat it. Ordinarily people would simply pop the raisin in their mouths, chew a few times and swallow, largely unconsciously. But mindful, meditative raisin eating is much different. It begins with looking intently at the raisin, considering its shape, weight, color and texture.

Next comes placing the raisin in the mouth, focusing on how it feels on the tongue as the mouth welcomes it with salivation. Then the mindful raisin-eater chews the raisin slowly and thoroughly, focusing on its taste and texture. Finally, swallowing the raisin involves following it all the way down to the stomach.

Once you commit to a mindfulness trigger-such as hanging up the phone, sipping a cup of tea or eating fruit snacks, starting the car or petting your dog-it's not difficult to work a dozen mindful moments into each day.

Journey Meditation

Journey meditation combines imagery and visualization to achieve a meditative state. This form of meditation appeals to those who find peace by picturing themselves in a peaceful place.

Here's how to do it.

Sit up straight. Get into a comfortable position. Either sit on the floor with your back against a wall, or sit in a chair with your feet on the ground and your hands resting on your knees or thighs. Have a pad and pencil nearby. Write down the worries, concerns or problems that you're afraid will distract you from meditation, and promise yourself that you'll deal with them when you're done.

Take a few cleansing breaths. Breathe in slowly and deeply for five counts, then exhale slowly for five counts.

Find a peaceful place. Close your eyes and concentrate on a soothing, tranquil place where you feel safe and calm. As distractions flutter through your mind, remind yourself that you'll deal with them when you are finished meditating.

A quiet beach is an ideal mental destination for most people. Picture yourself resting on the sand. Feel the sun on your skin, hear the water lapping the shore, listen for the sounds of seagulls or see the ships gliding out to sea. You can use the same routine for any beautiful, serene place that calms you.

Do it twice a day. Most persons will benefit from a 5- to 15-minute meditation practiced several days a week. A good rule of thumb for practicing journey meditation is to do it in the morning and then again later in the day. A peaceful meditative journey as you wake up can improve the whole tone of your day.

Journey meditation is also an excellent antidote for afternoon slump. Most people find that at about 3.00 PM, they are at their lowest energy level for the day. This is a good time to take a short nap or to take a short journey break. In as little as ten minutes, you'll find that you've refreshed yourself.

Body Scan Meditation

Body Scan Meditation is often used by people who want to try a more formal type of mindfulness without attending a yoga or tai chi class.

Lie on your back with your legs uncrossed, your arms at your sides, palms up, and your eyes open or closed, as you wish.
Focus on your breathing, how the air moves in and out of your body.

After several deep breaths, as you begin to feel comfortable and relaxed, direct your attention to the toes of your left foot. Tune into any sensations in that part of your body while remaining aware of your breathing. It often helps to imagine each breath flowing to the spot where you're directing your attention. Focus on your left toes for one to two minutes.

Then move your focus to the sole of your left foot and hold it there for a minute or two while continuing to pay attention to your breathing.

Follow the same procedure as you move to your left ankle, calf, knee, thigh, hip and so on all around the body.

Pay particular attention to any areas that cause pain or are the focus of any medical condition (for asthma, the lungs; for diabetes, the pancreas).

Pay particular attention to the head: the jaw, chin, lips, tongue, roof of the mouth, nostrils, throat, cheeks, eyelids, eyes, eyebrows, forehead, temples and scalp.

Finally, focus on the very top of your hair, the uppermost part of your body. Then let go of the body altogether, and in your mind, hover above yourself as your breath reaches beyond you and touches the universe.

The Instant Calming Sequence

Meditation and mindfulness are great when you have enough control over your time to enjoy them. But what happens when a crisis requires immediate action?

Using scientific findings in the physiology of relaxation, Dr. Robert Cooper has developed a six-step program that minimizes the negative effects of stress the moment the body begins to feel stressed. He calls it the Instant Calming Sequence.

Step 1: Practice uninterrupted breathing. When stress strikes, immediately focus on your breath and continue breathing smoothly, deeply and evenly.

Step 2: Put on a positive face. Smile a grin that you can feel in the corners of your eyes. "The conventional wisdom is that happiness triggers smiling," Dr. Cooper explains. "But recent studies suggest that this process is a two-way street. Smiling can contribute to feelings of happiness, and in a stressful situation, it can help keep you calm." Try this simple test: Smile a broad grin right now. Don't you feel better?

Step 3: Balance your posture. People under stress often look hunched-over, hence the oft-repeated phrase "They have the weight of the world on their shoulders."

"Maintaining good posture works like smiling," Dr. Cooper says. "Physical balance contributes to emotional balance." Keep your head up, chin in, chest high, pelvis and hips level, back comfortably straight and abdomen free of tension. Imagine a skyhook lifting your body from a point at the center of the top of your head.

Step 4: Bathe in a wave of relaxation. Consciously sweep a wave of relaxation through your body. "Imagine you're standing under a waterfall that washes away all your tension," Dr. Cooper says.

Step 5: Acknowledge reality. Face your causes of stresses head-on. Don't try to deny it or wish that it hadn't happened. Think: "This is real. I can handle it. I'm finding the best possible way to cope right now."

Step 6: Reassert control. Instead of fretting about how the stressor has robbed you of control, focus on what you can control and take appropriate action. Also, think clear-headed, honest thoughts instead of distorted ones.

Five Meditation Steps

Sitting comfortably but upright, feel your weight on the chair or cushion and relax into it. Imagine breathing in and out through your navel, taking a few deep breaths to settle in. Let your attention gather at a point at the base of your spine, imagine it as a point of energy. Notice what sensations you feel there.

Move your attention to the crown of the head. Imagine a point of energy there. Notice what sensations you feel. Feel these two points align, connected by a line of light, inside the body near the spine. Allow energy to move freely between these two points.

Let your attention come to rest at a point of balance along this line, deep within you, at the center of your being.

From this center of your being, imagine the line of light extending downward through your legs and feet, relaxing the toes and sinking into the earth. Breathing out, let all tension and fatigue run down this line into the earth.

Breathing in, imagine drawing up, through the soles of your feet, fresh, transformed earth energy. Allow it to fill your whole body from the feet up to the crown of your head, bringing a feeling of being supported and cradled by the solidity of the earth. Return your attention and your breathing to the center of your being. Imagine the line of light rising to the crown of your head and above, out into the clear blue sky, to the heavens. Breathe in fresh air.

Allow light and clearness from the heavens to radiate down the line of light to fill the whole body. Breathe into the center of your being and feel the two energies, from the earth and the sky, mingling. From this center let your attention be on your breath moving in and out (using one of the focuses suggested above).

Taoist Meditation Methods

Taoist meditation methods have many points in common with Hindu and Buddhist systems, but the Taoist way is less abstract and far more down-to-earth than the contemplative traditions which evolved in India. The primary hallmark of Taoist meditation is the generation, transformation, and circulation of internal energy.

Once the meditator has 'achieved energy' (deh-chee), it can be applied to promoting health and longevity, nurturing the 'spiritual embryo' of immortality, martial arts, healing, painting and poetry, sensual self-indulgence, or whatever else the adept wishes to do with it.

The two primary guidelines in Taoist meditation are jing ('quiet, stillness, calm') and ding ('concentration, focus'). The purpose of stillness, both mental and physical, is to turn attention inwards and cut off external sensory input, thereby muzzling the "Five Thieves". Within that silent stillness, one concentrates the mind and focuses attention, usually on the breath, in order to develop what is called 'one-pointed awareness', a totally undistracted, undisturbed, undifferentiated state of mind which permits intuitive insights to arise spontaneously.

Taoist masters suggest that when you first begin to practice meditation, you will find that your mind is very uncooperative. That's your ego, or 'emotional mind', fighting against its own extinction by the higher forces of spiritual awareness. The last thing your ego and emotions want is to be harnessed: they revel in the day-to-day circus of sensory entertainment and emotional turmoil, even though this game depletes your energy, degenerates your body, and exhausts your spirit. When you catch your mind drifting into fantasy or drawing attention away from internal alchemy to external phenomena, here are six ways you can use to 'catch the monkey', clarify the mind, and re-establish the internal focus:

Shift attention back to the inflow and outflow of air streaming through the nostrils, or energy streaming in and out of a vital point, such as between the brows.

Focus attention on the rising and falling of the navel, the expansion and contraction of the abdomen, as you breathe.

With eyes half-closed, focus vision on a candle flame or a mandala (geometric meditation picture). Focus on the center of the flame or picture, but also take in the edges with peripheral vision. The concentration required to do this usually clears all other distractions from the mind.

Practice a few minutes of mantra, the 'sacred syllables' which harmonize energy and focus the mind. Though mantras are usually associated with Hindu and Tibetan Buddhist practices, Taoists have also employed them for many millennia. The three most effective syllables are 'Om', which stabilizes the body, 'ah', which harmonizes energy, and 'hum', which concentrates the spirit. 'Om' vibrates between the brows, 'ah' in the throat, and 'hum' in the heart, and their associated colors are white, red, and blue respectively. Chant the syllables in a deep, low-pitched tone and use long, complete exhalations for each one. Other mantras are equally effective.

Beat the 'Heavenly Drum' as a cool-down energy-collection technique. The vibrations tend to clear discursive thoughts and sensory distractions from the mind.

Visualize a deity or a sacred symbol of personal significance to you shining above the crown of your head or suspended in space before you. When your mind is once again still, stable, and undistracted, let the vision fade away and refocus your mind on whatever meditative technique you were practicing.

Taoist meditation works on all three levels of the 'Three Treasures': essence (body), energy (breath), and spirit (mind).

The first step is to adopt a comfortable posture for the body, balance your weight evenly, straighten the spine, and pay attention to physical sensations such as heat, cold, tingling, trembling, or whatever else arises.

When your body is comfortable and balanced, shift attention to the second level, which is breath and energy. You may focus on the breath itself as it flows in and out of the lungs through the nostrils, or on energy streaming in and out of a particular point in tune with the breath.

The third level is spirit: when the breath is regulated and energy is flowing smoothly through the channels, focus attention on thoughts and feelings forming and dissolving in your mind, awareness expanding and contracting with each breath, insights and inspirations arising spontaneously, visions and images appearing and disappearing. Eventually you may even be rewarded with intuitive flashes of insight regarding the ultimate nature of the mind: open and empty as space; clear and luminous as a cloudless sky at sunrise; infinite and unimpeded.

Just as all the rules of chee-gung practice can be boiled down to the three Ss - slow, soft, smooth

- so the main points of meditation practice may be summed up in the three Cs: calm, cool, clear. As for proper postures for practice, the two positions most frequently used in Taoist meditation are (See the description of postures given elsewhere):

Sitting cross-legged on the floor in 'half-lotus' position, with the buttocks elevated on a cushion or pad. The advantages of this method are that this position is more stable and encourages energy to flow upwards towards the brain.

Sitting erect on a low stool or chair, feet parallel and shoulder width apart, knees bent at a 90-degree angle, spine erect. The advantages of sitting on a stool are that the legs do not cramp, the soles of the feet are in direct contact with the energy of the earth, and internal energy tends to flow more freely throughout the lower as well as the upper torso.

Most meditators who follow Taoist Meditation use both methods, depending on conditions. When sitting cross-legged, Western practitioners, whose legs tend to cramp more easily than Asians', are advised to sit on thick firm cushions, perhaps with a phone book or two underneath, in order to elevate the pelvis and take pressure off the legs and knees. This also helps keep the spine straight without straining the lower back.

The way the hands are placed is also important. The most natural and comfortable position is to rest the palms lightly on the thighs, just above the knees. However, some meditators find it more effective to use one of the traditional 'mudras', or hand gestures. Experiment with different combinations of posture and mudra until you find the style that suits you best.

Taoist meditation masters teach three basic ways to control the Fire mind of emotion with the Water mind of intent, so that the adept's goals in meditation may be realized.

The first method is called 'stop and observe'. This involves paying close attention to how thoughts arise and fade in the mind, learning to let them pass like a freight train in the night, without clinging to any particular one.

This develops awareness of the basic emptiness of all thought, as well as non-attachment to the rise and fall of emotional impulses. Gradually one learns simply to ignore the intrusion of discursive thoughts, at which point they cease arising for sheer lack of attention.

The second technique is called 'observe and imagine', which refers to visualization. The adept employs intent to visualize an image - such as Buddha, Jesus, a sacred symbol, the moon, a star, or whatever - in order to shift mental focus away from thoughts and emotions and stabilize the mind in one-pointed awareness.

You may also visualize a particular energy center in your body, or listen to the real or imagined sound of a bell, gong, or cymbal ringing in your ears. The point of focus is not important: what counts is shifting the focus of your attention away from idle thoughts, conflicting emotions, fantasies, and other distracting antics of the 'monkey mind' and concentrating attention instead on a stable point of focus established by the mind of intent, or 'wisdom mind'.

The third step in cultivating control over your own mind is called 'using the mind of intent to guide energy'. When the emotional mind is calm and the breath is regulated, focus attention on the internal energy. Learn how to guide it through the meridian network in order to energize vital organs, raise energy from the sacrum to the head to nourish the spirit and brain, and exchange stale energy for fresh energy from the external sources of heaven (sky) and earth (ground).

Begin by focusing attention on the Lower Elixir Field below the abdomen, then moving energy from there down to the perineum, up through the coccyx, and up along the spinal centers into the head, after which attention shifts to the Upper Elixir Field between the brows.

Though this sounds rather vague and esoteric to the uninitiated, a few months of practice, especially in conjunction with chee-gung and proper dietary habits, usually suffices to unveil the swirling world of energy and awareness hidden within our bodies and minds. All you have to do is sit still and shut up long enough for your mind to become aware of it.

It's always a good idea to warm up your body and open your energy channels with some chee-gung exercises before you sit down to meditate. This facilitates internal energy circulation and enables you to sit for longer periods without getting stiff or numb.

After sitting, you should avoid bathing for at least twenty minutes in order to prevent loss of energy through open pores and energy points. If you live in the northern hemisphere, it's best to sit facing south or east, in the general direction of the sun; in the southern hemisphere, sit facing north or east.

Given below are three Taoist meditations that are useful for beginners.

Taoist Meditation: Breath and Navel Meditation

Breath and Navel Meditation is the oldest meditation method on record in China as well as

India, and it is the method usually taught to beginners. Breath and Navel Meditation works directly with the natural flow of breath in the nostrils and the expansion and contraction of the abdomen. This Taoist meditation is a good way to develop focused attention and one-pointed awareness.

Method:

Sit cross-legged on a cushion on the floor or upright on a low stool and adjust the body's posture until well balanced and comfortable. Press tongue to palate, close your mouth without clenching the teeth, and lower the eyelids until almost closed.

Breathe naturally through the nose, drawing the inhalation deep down into the abdomen and making the exhalation long and smooth. Focus your attention on two sensations, one above and the other below. Above, focus on the gentle breeze of air flowing in and out of the nostrils like a bellows, and on exhalation try to 'follow' the breath out as far as possible, from 3 to 18 inches.

Below, focus on the navel rising and falling and the entire abdomen expanding and contracting like a balloon with each inhalation and exhalation. You may focus attention on the nostrils or the abdomen, or on both, or on one and then the other, whichever suits you best.

From time to time, mentally check your posture and adjust it if necessary. Whenever you catch your mind wandering off or getting cluttered with thoughts, consciously shift your attention back to your breath.

Sometimes it helps to count either inhalations or exhalations, until your mind is stably focused. If you manage to achieve stability in this method after ten to twenty minutes of practice, you may wish to switch over to one of the other two methods given below. All three of these methods may be practiced in a single sitting in the order that they are presented here, or in separate sittings.

Time: Twenty to thirty minutes, once or twice a day.

Taoist Meditation: Master Han's Central Channel Meditation

This is an ancient Taoist method modified and taught by Master Han Yu-mo at his Sung Yang Tao Centers in Taiwan and Canada. It is a simple and effective way for beginners rapidly to develop a tangible awareness of internal energy and a familiarity with the major power points through which energy is circulated and exchanged with the surrounding sources of heaven and earth. It relaxes the body, replenishes energy, and invigorates the spirit.

Method:

Adopt a comfortable sitting posture.

First, take a deep breath and bend forward slowly, exhaling audibly through the mouth in order to expel stale breath from the lungs; repeat three times.

Then sit still and breathe naturally, letting the abdomen expand and contract with each breath. However, instead of focusing attention on the flow of air through the nostrils, focus on the beam of energy entering the crown of the head at a point about two inches above the hairline, called the 'Medicine Palace'.

Feel the beam of energy flowing in through this point as you begin each inhalation and follow it down through the Central Channel into the Lower Elixir Field below the navel, then follow it back up the Central Channel and out through the Medicine Palace point on exhalation. The sensation at the crown point is most noticeable at the beginning of inhalation and the end of exhalation and feels somewhat like a flap or valve opening and closing as energy flows through it. There may also be feelings of warmth, tingling, or numbness in the scalp, all of which are signs of energy moving under the scrutiny of awareness.

After practicing this method for a few weeks or months and developing a conscious feel for energy as it moves through the Medicine Palace point, you may start to work with other points of exit during exhalation, always drawing energy in through the crown point on inhalation.

For example, you may bring energy in through the crown and down to the abdomen on inhalation, then push it back up and out through the 'Celestial Eye' point between the brows. This point usually brings rapid results - a distinct tingling or throbbing sensation between the brows. The Celestial Eye is the point through which adepts with 'psychic vision' perceive aspects of the world that are hidden to ordinary eyesight.

The mass of magnetite crystals between the forehead and the pituitary gland is sensitive to subtle fluctuations in surrounding electromagnetic fields. In other words, psychic vision perceives by virtue of its sensitivity to electromagnetic energy rather than the light or sound energy perceived by eyes and ears.

So-called 'psychics' are those who have learned how to interpret the electromagnetic signals from the magnetic organ between the eyes in terms of ordinary perception and rational thought.

In addition to the brow point, you may also practice expelling energy on exhalation through the points in the centers of the palms, the centers of the soles, and the perineum point midway between genitals and anus. In each case, look for sensations of warmth or tingling at the point of exit.

After practicing this method for a while, your head may start to rock spontaneously back and forth or from side to side after fifteen or twenty minutes of sitting, or else your entire body may start trembling and shaking. This is a good sign, for it means that your channels are opening and that energy is coursing strongly through them. Try neither to suppress nor encourage these sponta- neous tremors; instead just let them run their course naturally.

Time: Twenty to forty minutes, once or twice a day, preferably around dawn and midnight.

Taoist Meditation: Microcosmic Orbit Meditation

This is the classic Taoist meditation method for refining, raising, and circulating internal energy via the 'orbit' formed by the 'Governing Channel' from perineum up to head and the

Conception Channel from head back down to perineum. Activating the Microcosmic Orbit is a key step that leads to more advanced practices.

Taoists believe that microcosmic orbit meditation fills the reservoirs of the Governing and Conception channels with energy, which is then distributed to all the major organ-energy meridians, thereby energizing the internal organs. It draws abundant energy up from the sacrum into the brain, thereby enhancing cerebral circulation of blood and stimulating secretions of vital neurochemicals.

It is also the first stage for cultivating the 'spiritual embryo' or 'golden elixir' of immortality, a process that begins in the lower abdomen and culminates in the mid-brain. This is probably the best of all Taoist methods for cultivating health and longevity while also 'opening the three passes' to higher spiritual awareness.

Taoists often refer things in symbolic languages. (See the section on Human anatomy from the Taoist perspective for a description of the symbolism used in referring to the human anatomy.) 'Opening the Three Passes' is another name for this meditation method and refers to the three critical junctions which pave the way for energy to travel up from the sacrum through the Governing Channel along the spine into the head.

Method:

The first step is to still the body, calm the mind, and regulate the breath. With this settled mind, sit alone in a quiet room, senses shut and eyelids lowered. Turn your attention within, and inwardly visualize a pocket of energy in the umbilical region; within it is a point of golden light, clear and bright, immaculately pure. Focus attention on the navel until you feel the 'pocket of energy' glowing in the umbilical region.

The breath through your nose will naturally become light and subtle, going out and in evenly and finely, continuously and quietly, gradually becoming slighter and subtler. When the feeling is stable and the energy there is full, use your mind to guide energy down to the perineum and back up through the aperture in the coccyx.

Steadily visualize this true energy as being like a small snake gradually passing through the nine apertures of the coccyx. When you feel the energy has gone through this pass, visualize this true energy rising up to where the ribs meet the spine, then going through this pass and right on up to the Jade Pillow, the back of the brain.

Then imagine your true spirit in the Nirvana Chamber in the center of the brain, taking in the energy. When this true energy goes through the Jade Pillow, press the tongue against the palate.

The head should move forward and tilt slightly upwards to help it. When you feel this true energy penetrating the Nirvana Chamber, this may feel hot or swollen. This means the pass has been cleared and the energy has reached the Nirvana Center.

Next, focus attention on the Celestial Eye between the eyebrows and draw energy forwards from the midbrain and out through the point between the brows. This may cause a tingling or throbbing sensation there. Then the center of the brows will throb - this means the Celestial Eye is about to open. Then move the spirit into the center of the brows and draw the true energy through the Celestial Eye.

If you see the eighteen thousand pores and three hundred and sixty joints of the whole body explode open all at once, each joint parting three-tenths of an inch, this is evidence of the opening of the Celestial Eye.

This is what is meant when it is said that when one pass opens all the passes open, and when one opening is cleared all the openings are cleared.

You may wish to stay and work with this point for a few minutes, before letting energy sink down through the palate and tongue into the throat to the heart. This may feel as though there is cool water going down the Multistoried Tower of the windpipe. Do not swallow; let it go down by itself, bathing the bronchial tubes.

Then the vital energy will bathe the internal organs and then return to the genitals. This is what is called return to the root.

From the heart, draw it down through the Middle Elixir Field in the solar plexus, past the navel, and down into the Ocean of Energy reservoir in the Lower Elixir Field, where energy gathers, mixes, and is reserved for internal circulation. Then begin another cycle up through the coccyx to the mid-spine behind the heart and up past the Jade Pillow into the brain.

Breathe naturally with your abdomen, and don't worry whether energy moves up or down on inhalation or exhalation; coordinate the flow of breath and energy in whatever manner suits you best. However, if you reach the stage where you can complete a full Microcosmic Orbit in a single breath, it's best to raise energy up from coccyx to head on exhalation and draw it down from Upper to Lower Elixir Field on inhalation.

If you practice this way for a long time, eventually you can complete a whole cycle of ascent and descent in one visualization. If you can quietly practice this inner work continuously, whether walking, standing still, sitting, or lying down, then the vital energy will circulate within, and there will naturally be no problem of leakage. Chronic physical ailments, Taoists believe, will naturally disappear.

Also, once the inner energy is circulating, the breath will naturally become fine, and the true positive energy of heaven and earth will be inhaled by way of the breath and go down to join your own generative energy. The two energies will mix together, both to be circulated by you together, descending and ascending over and over, circulating up and down to replenish the depleted true energy in your body.

This true energy harmonizes and reforms, so that the vital fluids produced by the energy of daily life again produce true vitality. When true vitality is fully developed, it naturally produces true energy, and when true energy is fully developed it naturally produces our true spirit.

If you have any physical problems or discomforts in a particular section of your body, focus your energy at the pass closest to the discomfort and let it throb there for a while. This will help heal and rejuvenate the injured tissues. For example, if you have pelvic problems, focus energy on the coccyx pass; for lower-back pain focus on the lowest lumbar vertebra just above the sacrum; for upper-back and shoulder pain focus on the fifth thoracic vertebra, and so forth.

This meditation may also cause the head to rock or the body to tremble, which Taoists believe, are signs of progress.

Time: Thirty to forty-five minutes, once or twice a day.

Tools For Relaxation

Meditation Music

There are a great many tools that can assist you in your meditation practice, and some can be very effective in helping to achieve deeper states of relaxation and awareness.

Meditation music is one such tool.

Soothing "new age" music works quite well, and there are many CD's available that are made specifically for meditation.

I prefer the music of Steven Halpern or Hans Engel.

"Fixed Tone" CD's are particularly effective for me, where the music centers around a fixed chord or tone that serves as a mantra, or "Om".

I find music containing drums, percussion, vocals or flute distracting, so I stick to purely instrumental music that does not contain these elements.

Binaural Beats and Brain Wave Entrainment

A fascinating area of brain wave and psycho-acoustic research are Binaural beats and Brain Wave Entrainment.

Binaural beats are auditory brainstem responses, which originate in the superior olivary nucleus of each hemisphere.

They result from the interaction of two different auditory impulses, originating in opposite ears, below 1000 Hz and which differ in frequency between one and 30 Hz (Oster, 1973).

For example, if a pure tone of 400 Hz is presented to the right ear and a pure tone of 410 Hz is presented simultaneously to the left ear, an amplitude modulated standing wave of 10 Hz, the difference between the two tones, is experienced as the two wave forms mesh in and out of phase within the superior olivary nuclei.

This binaural beat is not heard in the ordinary sense of the word (the human range of hearing is from 20-20,000 Hz). It is perceived as an auditory beat and theoretically can be used to entrain specific neural rhythms through the frequency-following response (FFR)--the tendency for cortical potentials to entrain to or resonate at the frequency of an external stimulus.

Thus, it is theoretically possible to utilize a specific binaural-beat frequency as a consciousness management technique to entrain a specific cortical rhythm.

These binaural beat frequencies are now featured in specially designed meditation-music programs to help the listener achieve higher states of awareness and deeper levels of relaxation.

You may want to experiment with a few of these to see if you experience some of the dramatic effects these programs are reported by many to have.

I use them regularly in my own meditation practice and find them to be especially soothing, particularly when going from the Theta state of deep relaxation down to the Delta state, where sleep occurs.

Yoga

While the practice of yoga is a separate subject and discipline than meditation, (and beyond the scope of this book), yoga can enhance the effectiveness of the meditative experience and can help greatly in achieving deeper meditative states.

For those unfamiliar with it, yoga is the practice of postures and stretching that help to build strength and flexibility through a series of exercises and breathing techniques.

The practice can be complex but a simple and effective introduction to basic yoga and can be learned easily through instructional video or from a local class or private instructor.

Many fitness centers offer inexpensive classes, and yoga instructors can be found locally in almost every area of the globe, no matter how remote.

Your local YMCA is also a great place to check for inexpensive classes near where you live.

If you are more comfortable learning yoga at home, I have included some resources for learn at home courses available on video that can be rented from your local video store, found at your local library, or purchased online.

The Setting: Lighting and Mood

I believe lighting and mood are important for the practice of meditation. I like to do it in a darkened room, with a few lit candles, low meditation music, some incense or scented oils in the air.

Naturally, you will want to make sure you are in an area where you won't be disturbed or distracted. Turn off your cell phone or regular house phone, and let your family members know you want to be left alone.

This is your retreat, your sanctuary. Treat it with a deep sense of reverence and devotion.

But keep in mind that even if you are not in an ideal environment, meditation can be done anywhere.

Meditation Anywhere

One of the great things about meditation is the fact it can be done anywhere: Standing in line at the grocery store or post office. Waiting in the doctor or dentist office. Sitting at your desk at the office. Waiting on hold on the phone. Even sitting at traffic light!

In fact, any of the times when we are placed in a position where we are apt to become impatient is a perfect time and place for meditation.

Meditation slows the frantic mind from its madhouse race to get to the "next thing." I read somewhere where the mind and its thoughts are like a monkey running through the jungle in search of the next vine.

This impatient and relentless inability to slow down and relax into the acceptance and experiencing the moment is exactly what meditation addresses.

It teaches patience, wisdom and calm detachment, the opposite of our natural tendency to frantically grab the next thought, thing or idea.

The truly beautiful thing about it is that it can be done anywhere, anytime, and for even a period of seconds it can be quite effective in calming and focusing the noisy and disturbed psyche.

Conclusion

Today we need meditation more than we ever did in history. With the modern world and technology and more responsibility to keep track of, our minds and bodies need peace and solace and relaxation from the stresses that abound.

This small, simple book has attempted to make this pursuit a little easier to understand, practice and accomplish, and to introduce the layperson simple meditation techniques that can be used for life.

Practice these techniques a little everyday, whether you only have a few seconds or you have an hour.

In these techniques you will find more patience, tolerance and peaceful bliss that will enrich your days and bring you great serenity for many years to come.

Recommended Meditation CD's/Music

Music For Relaxation and Deep Meditation –
    MindWaves (with binaural beats)
Music for Healing - Steven Halpern
Reiki Hands of Light - Deuter
Eternal Now - Don Peyote
Deep Journeys - Steven Halpern
Yoga Zone - Music For Meditation -
    Various Artists
Yearning - Robert Rich and Lisa Maslow
Beyond Body and Mind - Karanush
Mental Clarity - Robert Haig Coxon

Recommended Meditation and Yoga Videos

Kundalini Yoga for Beginners & Beyond -
    Ana Brett and Ravi Singh
Yoga Shakti - Shiva Rea
Breathe: Kundalini Yoga with Harijiwan -
    Harijiwan Khalsa
Meditation for Beginners - Maritza
Relaxation & Breathing for Meditation -
    Rodney Yee

Mindfulness Meditation and Stress Reduction for Beginners: The Garden of NOW - Derek G. Turesky

Recommended Reading

Meditation for Beginners - Jack Kornfield
8 Minute Meditation: Quiet Your Mind. Change Your Life - Victor Davich
Opening to Meditation: A Gentle, Guided Approach (Book & CD) - Diana Lang

Website Resources

Learning Meditation
http://www.learningmeditation.com/

How To Meditate
http://www.how-to-meditate.org/

The Meditation Center
http://www.meditationcenter.com/

Zen and Meditation For Beginners
http://zenhabits.net/